Sawyer

NORTH
AMERICA

ASKA

CALIFORNIA

QUEBEC
CHICAGO   •BOSTON

LOUISIANA
FLORIDA

YUCATAN
GUATEMALA   JAMAICA
HONDURAS

PERU

SOUTH
AMERICA

A T L A N T I C   O C E A N

LONDON
EUROPE

AFRICA

3:00 4:00 5:00 6:00 7:00 8:00 9:00 10:00 11:00 12:00 1:00 2:00

SOMEWHERE IN THE WORLD RIGHT NOW

by Stacey Schuett

SCHOLASTIC INC.
New York Toronto London Auckland Sydney

To Mavis and Frances,
for seeing beyond the horizon

ISBN 0-590-44088-8

12 11 10 9 8 7 6 5 4 3 2 1   8 9/9 0 1 2 3/0

Printed in the U.S.A.   14

First Scholastic printing, January 1998

A Note to the Reader

The earth is constantly turning on its axis. One full rotation takes 24 hours, and during that time, the position of the sun in the sky changes, creating light and dark, day and night.

It used to be that many places measured time from when the sun was highest overhead, at noon. But this meant that neighboring cities would have different clock times at the same instant. Faster travel and better communications made this inconvenient, so in 1884 an international agreement was reached to adopt a system of standard times. The planet was divided into 24 equal areas called time zones. (However, as the maps on the endpapers show, the time zones were adjusted to conform to geographical and political boundaries.) Everywhere within each zone, it is always the same time. When moving from one time zone to the next, there is a change in one hour, forward or backward, depending on whether one is moving east or west.

An important feature of the time zone system is the international date line. As the sun crosses the 24 time zones, somewhere a change in date must occur. The international community needed to agree on a boundary where the new date would begin. It's clear that to have the date change in the middle of a crowded country would cause much confusion, so the line was drawn through the Pacific Ocean, with a few jogs around inhabited regions. Since the earth turns eastward, places west of the date line move into the new date first. So, no matter where in the world you are, there's somewhere else where it's a different day!

*S*omewhere in the world right now, it's deepest night. Fog hugs the shoulders of buildings and bridges. A baker slides long loaves of bread into an oven. Somewhere, somebody watches a movie. A mouse hunts for crumbs.

Somewhere else, in velvety darkness, elephants sleep standing up, swaying gently from side to side.

Whales breach and dive in the sea, singing their low, sweet songs. Penguins press close to their chicks to keep them warm.

Somewhere, the night wind sighs and murmurs. The moon shines through a window. A little girl lies dreaming of tomorrow.

But somewhere else, right now, tomorrow is already here. Dawn is breaking. A rooster crows and people are waking up.

BHUTAN

Somewhere, it's morning. Families eat breakfast. Kids get dressed for school. Farmers leave for the fields to tend their crops.

Birds stretch their wings and sing. A boy hides
a note for a friend to find. People go to work,
stores open . . . another day has begun.

And somewhere, right now, people buy food for their midday meal. A carpenter measures wood. A dog runs off with his lunch.

In the late morning shade, a baby kangaroo naps. A koala munches eucalyptus leaves.

Somewhere in the world right now, fishing boats return with their catch. Sea gulls swoop and dive and bicker over scraps.

Somewhere, the afternoon sun gilds workers in the vineyards. Cows graze and rest in the grass. A girl tends her horses.

Somewhere in the world right now, the sun
is setting. Monkeys screech from the trees
as a jaguar glides through the jungle. Parrots
mutter and chuckle. Shadows grow long.

North Chicago
Lake Forest
Highland Park
Winnetka
Wilmette
Evanston

CHICAGO
E.
Chicago

And somewhere else, the sun has already slipped away, drawing evening down like a shade. In the city, signs flash on and off, off and on. Trains whoosh through tunnels, taking people home.

Somewhere, suddenly, houses light up. A girl and her
brother race each other to the door.

The day's work is done. A family sits down to supper.

And somewhere else, night has fallen. Clouds
cushion the moon as it climbs across the sky.
An alligator sleeps in an inky swamp beneath
a tapestry of stars.

The last notes of a song fade into the rhythm of the waves.

Somewhere, a truck driver follows her headlights
down a lonely road. A night watchman starts his shift.

Friends say good night.

Somewhere, somebody reads a story, and someone listens.

Brookline

Voices whisper, "Sweet dreams," and under a blanket of night, lights go out one by one, somewhere in the world . . .

right now.

EUROPE

RUSSIA

ASIA

CHINA

BHUTAN

INDIA

AFRICA

UGANDA
KENYA

MADAGASCAR

INDIAN

OCEAN

QUEENSLAND

AUSTRALIA

PAO
O

MONDAY
SUNDAY

INTERNATIONAL DATE LINE

MONDAY
SUNDAY

ANTARCTICA

00 3:00 4:00 5:00 6:00 7:00 8:00 9:00 10:00 11:00 12:00 1:00